THREE PLAYS

OHIO IMPROMPTU

CATASTROPHE

WHAT WHERE

Works by Samuel Beckett
Published by Grove Press

Cascando and Other Short Dramatic Pieces
(Words and Music; Eh Joe; Come and Go; Film [original version])
Collected Poems in English and French
The Collected Shorter Plays of Samuel Beckett
The Collected Works of Samuel Beckett (twenty-five volumes)
Company
Disjecta: Miscellaneous Writings and a Dramatic Fragment
Endgame
Ends and Odds
(Not I; That Time; Footfalls; Ghost Trio; . . . but the clouds . . . ; Theatre I;
Theatre II; Radio I; Radio II)
Film, a Film Script
First Love and Other Shorts
(From an Abandoned Work; Enough; Imagination Dead Imagine; Ping;
Not I; Breath)
Fizzles
Happy Days
How It Is
I Can't Go On, I'll Go On: A Selection from Samuel Beckett's Work
Ill Seen Ill Said
Krapp's Last Tape and Other Dramatic Pieces
(All That Fall; Embers [a play for radio]; Acts Without Words I and II
[mimes])
The Lost Ones
Malone Dies
Mercier and Camier
Molloy
More Pricks Than Kicks
Murphy
Ohio Impromptu, Catastrophe, and What Where: Three Plays
Poems in English
Proust
Rockaby and Other Works
(Ohio Impromptu; All Strange Away; A Piece of Monologue)
Stories and Texts for Nothing
Three Novels
(Molloy; Malone Dies; The Unnamable)
The Unnamable
Waiting for Godot
Watt
Worstward Ho

THREE PLAYS

OHIO IMPROMPTU
CATASTROPHE
WHAT WHERE

by Samuel Beckett

GROVE PRESS, INC./New York

First Hardcover Edition 1984
First Printing 1984
ISBN: 0-394-53851-X
Library of Congress Catalog Card Number: 83-49372

First Evergreen Edition 1984
First Printing 1984
ISBN: 0-394-62061-5
Library of Congress Catalog Card Number: 83-49372

Printed in the United States of America

GROVE PRESS, INC., 196 West Houston Street,
New York, N.Y. 10014

5   4   3   2   1

Ohio Impromptu

Ohio Impromptu was first performed in the Drake Union, Stadium 2 Theatre, in association with Ohio State University, on May 9, 1981. It was directed by Alan Schneider.

Reader	David Warrilow
Listener	Rand Mitchell

●

Ohio Impromptu was produced by Lucille Lortel and The Harold Clurman Theatre, New York, New York, on June 15, 1983. It was directed by Alan Schneider.

Reader	David Warrilow
Listener	Rand Mitchell

L = *Listener.*

R = *Reader.*

As alike in appearance as possible.

Light on table midstage. Rest of stage in darkness. Plain white deal table, say 8' x 4'. Two plain armless white deal chairs.

L *seated at table facing front towards end of long side audience right. Bowed head propped on right hand. Face hidden. Left hand on table. Long black coat. Long white hair.*

R *seated at table in profile centre of short side audience right. Bowed head propped on right hand. Left hand on table. Book on table before him open at last pages. Long black coat. Long white hair.*

Black wide-brimmed hat at centre of table.

Fade up.

Ten seconds.

R *turns page.*
Pause.

R *(reading)***:** Little is left to tell. In a last—

L *knocks with left hand on table.*

Little is left to tell.

Pause. Knock.

In a last attempt to obtain relief he moved from where they had been so long together to a single room on the far bank. From its single window he could see the downstream extremity of the Isle of Swans.

Pause.

Relief he had hoped would flow from unfamiliarity. Unfamiliar room. Unfamiliar scene. Out to where nothing ever shared. Back to where nothing ever shared. From this he had once half hoped some measure of relief might flow.

Pause.

Day after day he could be seen slowly pacing the islet. Hour after hour. In his long black coat no matter what the weather and old world Latin Quarter hat. At the tip he would always pause to dwell on the receding stream. How in joyous eddies its two arms conflowed and flowed united on. Then turn and his slow steps retrace.

Pause.

In his dreams—

Knock.

Then turn and his slow steps retrace.

Pause. Knock.

In his dreams he had been warned against this change. Seen the dear face and heard the unspoken words, Stay where we were so long alone together, my shade will comfort you.

Pause.

Could he not—

Knock.

Seen the dear face and heard the unspoken words, Stay where we were so long alone together, my shade will comfort you.

Pause. Knock.

Could he not now turn back? Acknowledge his error and return to where they were once so long alone together. Alone together so much shared. No. What he had done alone could not be undone. Nothing he had ever done alone could ever be undone. By him alone.

Pause.

In this extremity his old terror of night laid hold on him again. After so long a lapse that as if never been. *(Pause. Looks closer.)* Yes, after so long a lapse that as if never been. Now with redoubled force the fearful symptoms described at length page forty paragraph four. *(Starts to turn back the pages. Checked by **L**'s left hand. Resumes relinquished page.)* White nights now again his portion. As when his heart was young. No sleep no braving sleep till—*(turns page)*—dawn of day.

Pause.

Little is left to tell. One night—

Knock.

Little is left to tell.

Pause. Knock.

One night as he sat trembling head in hands
from head to foot a man appeared to him and
said, I have been sent by—and here he named
the dear name—to comfort you. Then drawing
a worn volume from the pocket of his long
black coat he sat and read till dawn. Then
disappeared without a word.

Pause.

Some time later he appeared again at the same
hour with the same volume and this time without
preamble sat and read it through again the long
night through. Then disappeared without a
word.

Pause.

So from time to time unheralded he would
appear to read the sad tale through again and
the long night away. Then disappear without a
word.

Pause.

With never a word exchanged they grew to be
as one.

Pause.

Till the night came at last when having closed
the book and dawn at hand he did not disappear
but sat on without a word.

Pause.

Finally he said, I have had word from— and
here he named the dear name—that I shall not
come again. I saw the dear face and heard the
unspoken words, No need to go to him again,
even were it in your power.

Pause.

So the sad—

Knock.

Saw the dear face and heard the unspoken words, No need to go to him again, even were it in your power.

Pause. Knock.

So the sad tale a last time told they sat on as though turned to stone. Through the single window dawn shed no light. From the street no sound of reawakening. Or was it that buried in who knows what thoughts they paid no heed? To light of day. To sound of reawakening. What thoughts who knows. Thoughts, no, not thoughts. Profounds of mind. Buried in who knows what profounds of mind. Of mindlessness. Whither no light can reach. No sound. So sat on as though turned to stone. The sad tale a last time told.

Pause.

Nothing is left to tell.

Pause. **R** *makes to close book.*

Knock. Book half-closed.

Nothing is left to tell.

Pause. **R** *closes book.*

Knock.

Silence. Five seconds.

Simultaneously they lower their right hands to table, raise their heads and look ut each other Unblinking. Expressionless.

Ten seconds.

Fade out.

Catastrophe

FOR VACLAV HAVEL

Catastrophe was first performed at The Avignon Festival, Avignon, France, on July 21, 1982. It was directed by Stephan Meldegg.

The Protagonist	Pierre Arditi
The Director	Gerard Desarthe
The Assistant	Stephanie Loik

•

Catastrophe was first produced in the United States by Lucille Lortel and The Harold Clurman Theatre, New York, New York, on June 15, 1983. It was directed by Alan Schneider.

Protagonist	David Warrilow
The Director	Donald Davis
His Assistant	Margaret Reed
Luke	Rand Mitchell

Director (D).

His female assistant (A).

Protagonist (P).

Luke, *in charge of the lighting, offstage* **(L).**

Rehearsal. Final touches to the last scene. Bare stage. **A** *and* **L** *have just set the lighting.* **D** *has just arrived.*

D *in an armchair downstage audience left. Fur coat. Fur toque to match. Age and physique unimportant.*

A *standing beside him. White overall. Bare head. Pencil on ear. Age and physique unimportant.*

P *midstage standing on a black block 18 inches high. Black wide-brimmed hat. Black dressing-gown to ankles. Barefoot. Head bowed. Hands in pockets. Age and physique unimportant.*

D *and* **A** *contemplate* **P***. Long pause.*

A: *(Finally).* Like the look of him?

D: So so. *(Pause.)* Why the plinth?

A: To let the stalls see the feet.

Pause.

D: Why the hat?

A: To help hide the face.

Pause.

D: Why the gown?

A: To have him all black.

Pause.

D: What has he on underneath? *(**A** moves towards **P**.)* Say it.

A *halts.*

A: His night attire.

D: Colour?

A: Ash.

D *takes out a cigar.*

D: Light. *(**A** returns, lights the cigar, stands still. **D** smokes.)* How's the skull?

A: You've seen it.

D: I forget. *(**A** moves towards **P**.)* Say it.

A *halts.*

A: Moulting. A few tufts.

D: Colour?

A: Ash.

Pause.

D: Why hands in pockets?

A: To help have him all black.

D: They mustn't.

A: I make a note. *(She takes out a pad, takes pencil, notes.)* Hands exposed.
She puts back pad and pencil.

D: How are they? *(A at a loss. Irritably.)* The hands, how are the hands?

A: You've seen them.

D: I forget.

A: Crippled. Fibrous degeneration.

D: Clawlike?

A: If you like.

D: Two claws?

A: Unless he clench his fists.

D: He mustn't.

A: I make a note. *(She takes out pad, takes pencil, notes.)* Hands limp.

She puts back pad and pencil.

D: Light. *(A returns, relights the cigar, stands still, D smokes.)* Good. Now let's have a look. *(A at a loss. Irritably.)* Get going. Lose that gown. *(He consults his chronometer.)* Step on it, I have a caucus.

A goes to P, takes off the gown. P submits, inert. A steps back, the gown over her arm. P in old grey pyjamas, head bowed, fists clenched. Pause.

A: Like him better without? *(Pause.)* He's shivering.

D: Not all that. Hat.

A *advances, takes off hat, steps back, hat in hand. Pause.*

A: Like that cranium?

D: Needs whitening.

A: I make a note. *(She takes out pad, takes pencil, notes.)* Whiten cranium.

She puts back pad and pencil.

D: The hands. *(**A** at a loss. Irritably.)* The fists. Get going. *(**A** advances, unclenches fists, steps back.)* And whiten.

A: I make a note. *(She takes out pad, takes pencil, notes.)* Whiten hands.

She puts back pad and pencil. They contemplate
P.

D: *(Finally)*. Something wrong. *(Distraught.)*
What is it?

A: *(Timidly)*. What if we were to . . . were
to . . . join them?

D: No harm trying. (**A** *advances, joins the
hands, steps back.)* Higher. (**A** *advances, raises
waist-high the joined hands, steps back.)* A
touch more. (**A** *advances, raises breast-high the
joined hands.)* Stop! *(**A** steps back.)* Better. It's
coming. Light.

A *returns, relights cigar, stands still.* **D** *smokes.*

A: He's shivering.

D: Bless his heart. *Pause.*

A: *(Timidly)*. What about a little . . . a little . . .
gag?

D: For God's sake! This craze for explication! Every i dotted to death! Little gag! For God's sake!

A: Sure he won't utter?

D: Not a squeak. *(He consults his chronometer.)* Just time. I'll go and see how it looks from the house.

Exit **D**, *not to appear again.* **A** *subsides in the armchair, springs to her feet no sooner seated, takes out a rag, wipes vigorously back and seat of chair, discards rag, sits again. Pause.*

D: *(Off, plaintive)*. I can't see the toes. *(Irritably)*. I'm sitting in the front row of the stalls and can't see the toes.

A: *(Rising)*. I make a note. *(She takes out pad, takes pencil, notes.)* Raise pedestal.

D: There's a trace of face.

A: I make a note.

She takes out pad, takes pencil, makes to note.

D: Down the head. *(A at a loss. Irritably.)* Get going. Down his head. *(A puts back pad and pencil, goes to* **P**, *bows his head further, steps back.)* A shade more. *(A advances, bows the head further.)* Stop! *(A steps back.)* Fine. It's coming. *(Pause.)* Could do with more nudity.

A: I make a note.

She takes out pad, makes to take pencil.

D: Get going! Get going! *(A puts back the pad, goes to* **P**, *stands irresolute.)* Bare the neck. *(A undoes top buttons, parts the flaps, steps back.)* The legs. The shins. *(A advances, rolls up to below knee one trouser-leg, steps back.)* The other. *(Same for other leg, steps back.)* Higher. The knees. *(A advances, rolls up to above knees both trouser-legs, steps back.)* And whiten.

● 33

A: I make a note. *(She takes out pad, takes pencil, notes.)* Whiten all flesh.

D: It's coming. Is Luke around?

A: *(Calling.)* Luke! *(Pause. Louder.)* Luke!

L: *(Off, distant)*. I hear you. *(Pause. Nearer.)* What's the trouble now?

A: Luke's around.

D: Blackout stage.

L: What?

A *transmits in technical terms. Fade-out of general light. Light on* **P** *alone.* **A** *in shadow.*

D: Just the head.

L: What?

A *transmits in technical terms. Fade-out of light
on* P's *body. Light on head alone. Long pause.*

D: Lovely. *Pause.*

A: *(Timidly).* What if he were to . . . were
to . . . raise his head . . . an instant . . . show his
face . . . just an instant.

D: For God's sake! What next? Raise his head!
Where do you think we are? In Patagonia?
Raise his head! For God's sake! *(Pause)* Good.
There's our catastrophe. In the bag. Once
more and I'm off.

A: *(to* L.*)* Once more and he's off.
Fade-up of light on P's *body. Pause. Fade-up of
general light.*

D: Stop! *(Pause.)* Now . . . let 'em have it.
*(Fade-out of general light. Pause. Fade-out of
light on body. Light on head alone. Long pause.)*

Terrific! He'll have them on their feet. I can
hear it from here.

*Pause. Distant storm of applause. **P** raises his
head, fixes the audience. The applause falters,
dies.*

Long pause.

Fade-out of light on face.

What Where

What Where was first produced by Lucille Lortel and The Harold Clurman Theatre, New York, New York, on June 15, 1983. It was directed by Alan Schneider.

Bam	Donald Davis
Bom	David Warrilow
Bim	Rand Mitchell
Bem	Daniel Wirth
Voice of Bam	Donald Davis

Bam
Bem
Bim
Bom
Voice of Bam (V)

Note.
Players as alike as possible.
Same long grey gown.
Same long grey hair.
V in the shape of a small megaphone at head
level.

Playing area (P) rectangle 3m x 2m, dimly lit,
surrounded by shadow, stage right as seen from
house. Downstage left, dimly lit, surrounded by
shadow, V.

General dark.
Light on V.
Pause.

V: We are the last five.
In the present as were we still.
It is spring.
Time passes.
First without words.
I switch on.

Light on P.
Bam *at 3 head haught,* **Bom** *at 1 head bowed.*
Pause.

Not good.
I switch off.

Light off P.

I start again.
We are the last five.
It is spring.
Time passes.
First without words.
I switch on.

Light on P.
Bam *alone at 3 head haught.*
Pause.

Good.
I am alone.
It is spring.
Time passes.
First without words.
In the end Bom appears.
Reappears.

Bom *enters at N, halts at 1 head bowed.*
Pause.
Bim *enters at E, halts at 2 head haught.*

Pause.
Bim *exits at E followed by* **Bom**.
Pause.
Bim *enters at E, halts at 2 head bowed.*
Pause.
Bem *enters at N, halts at 1 head haught.*
Pause.

Bem *exits at N followed by* **Bim**.
Pause.
Bem *enters at N, halts at 1 head bowed.*
Pause.
Bam *exits at W followed by* **Bem**.
Pause.
Bam *enters at W, halts at 3 head bowed.*
Pause.

Good.
I switch off.

Light off P.

I start again.
We are the last five.
It is spring.
Time passes.
I switch on.

Light on P.
Bam *alone at 3 head haught.*
Pause.

Good.
I am alone.
It is spring.
Time passes.
Now with words.
In the end Bom appears.
Reappears.

Bom *enters at N, halts at I head bowed.*

Bam: Well?

Bom: *(Head bowed throughout).* Nothing.

Bam: He didn't say anything?

Bom: No.

Bam: You gave him the works?

Bom: Yes.

Bam: And he didn't say anything?

Bom: No.

Bam: He wept?

Bom: Yes.

Bam: Screamed?

Bom: Yes.

Bam: Begged for mercy?

Bom: Yes.

Bam: But didn't say anything?

Bom: No.

V: Not good.
I start again.

Bam: Well?

Bom: Nothing.

Bam: He didn't say it?

V: Good.

Bom: No.

Bam: You gave him the works?

Bom: Yes.

Bam: And he didn't say it?

Bom: No.

Bam: He wept?

Bom: Yes.

Bam: Screamed?

Bom: Yes.

Bam: Begged for mercy?

Bom: Yes.

Bam: But didn't say it?

Bom: No.

Bam: Then why stop?

Bom: He passed out.

Bam: And you didn't revive him?

Bom: I tried.

Bam: Well?

Bom: I couldn't.

Pause.

Bam: It's a lie. *(Pause.)* He said it to you. *(Pause.)* Confess he said it to you. *(Pause.)* You'll be given the works until you confess.

V: Good.
In the end Bim appears.

Bim *enters at E, halts at 2 head haught.*

Bam: *(to* **Bim***).* Are you free?

Bim: Yes.

Bam: Take him away and give him the works until he confesses.

Bim: What must he confess?

Bam: That he said it to him.

Bim: Is that all?

Bam: Yes.

V: Not good.
I start again.

Bam: Take him away and give him the works until he confesses.

Bim: What must he confess?

Bam: That he said it to him.

Bim: Is that all?

Bam: And what.

V: Good.

Bim: Is that all?

Bam: Yes.

Bim: Then stop?

Bam: Yes.

Bim: Good. *(To* **Bom.***)* Come.

Bim *exits at E followed by* **Bom**.

V: Good.
I am alone.
It is summer.
Time passes.
In the end Bim appears.
Reappears.

Bim *enters at E, halts at 2 head bowed.*

Bam: Well?

Bim: *(Head bowed throughout)*. Nothing.

Bam: He didn't say it?

Bim: No.

Bam: You gave him the works?

Bim: Yes.

Bam: And he didn't say it?

Bim: No.

V: Not good.
I start again.

Bam: Well?

Bim: Nothing.

Bam: He didn't say where?

V: Good.

Bim: Where?

V: Ah!

Bam: Where.

Bim: No.

Bam: You gave him the works?

Bim: Yes.

Bam: And he didn't say where?

Bim: No.

Bam: He wept?

Bim: Yes.

Bam: Screamed?

Bim: Yes.

Bam: Begged for mercy?

Bim: Yes.

Bam: But didn't say where?

Bim: No.

Bam: Then why stop?

Bim: He passed out.

Bam: And you didn't revive him?

Bim: I tried.

Bam: Well?

Bim: I couldn't.

Pause.

Bam: It's a lie. *(Pause.)* He said where to you.
(Pause.) Confess he said where to you. *(Pause.)*
You'll be given the works until you confess.

V: Good.
In the end Bem appears.

Bem *enters at N, halts at l head haught.*

Bam: *(to Bem)*. Are you free?

Bem: Yes.

Bam: Take him away and give him the works until he confesses.

Bem: What must he confess?

Bam: That he said where to him.

Bem: Is that all?

Bam: Yes.

V: Not good.
I start again.

Bam: Take him away and give him the works until he confesses.

Bem: What must he confess?

Bam: That he said where to him.

Bem: Is that all?

Bam: And where.

V: Good.

Bem: Is that all?

Bam: Yes.

Bem: Then stop?

Bam: Yes.

Bem: Good. *(To* **Bim**.*)* Come.

Bem *exits at N followed by* **Bim**.

V: Good.

I am alone.
It is autumn.
Time passes.
In the end Bem appears.
Reappears.

Bem *enters at N, halts at 1 head bowed.*

Bam: Well?

Bem: *(Head bowed throughout).* Nothing.

Bam: He didn't say where?

Bem: No.

V: So on.

Bam: It's a lie. *(Pause.)* He said where to you.
(Pause.) Confess he said where to you. *(Pause.)*
You'll be given the works until you confess.

Bem: What must I confess?

Bam: That he said where to you.

Bem: Is that all?

Bam: And where.

Bem: Is that all?

Bam: Yes.

Bem: Then stop?

Bam: Yes. Come.

Bam *exits at W followed by* **Bem**.

V: Good.
It is winter.
Time passes.
In the end I appear.
Reappear.

Bam *enters at N, halts at 3 head bowed.*

V: Good.
I am alone.
In the present as were I still.
It is winter.
Without journey.
Time passes.
That is all.
Make sense who may.
I switch off.

Light off P.
Pause.
Light off V.

OTHER GROVE PRESS DRAMA AND THEATER PAPERBACKS

17016-4 MAMET, DAVID / American Buffalo / $4.95
17040-7 MAMET, DAVID / A Life in the Theatre / $6.95
17043-1 MAMET, DAVID / Sexual Perversity in Chicago and The Duck Variations / $5.95
17264-7 MROZEK, SLAWOMIR / Tango / $3.95
17092-X ODETS, CLIFFORD / Six Plays (Waiting for Lefty; Awake and Sing; Golden Boy; Rocket to the Moon; Till the Day I Die; Paradise Lost) / $7.95
17001-6 ORTON, JOE / The Complete Plays (The Ruffian on the Stair, The Good and Faithful Servant, The Erpingham Camp, Funeral Games, Loot, What the Butler Saw, Entertaining Mr. Sloane) / $6.95
17019-9 PINTER, HAROLD / Complete Works: One (The Birthday Party, The Room, The Dumb Waiter, A Slight Ache, A Night Out, The Black and White, The Examination) / $6.95
17020-2 PINTER, HAROLD / Complete Works: Two (The Caretaker, Night School, The Dwarfs, The Collection, The Lover, Five Revue Sketches) / $6.95
17251-5 PINTER, HAROLD / The Homecoming / $4.95
17885-8 PINTER, HAROLD / No Man's Land / $3.95
17539-5 POMERANCE, BERNARD / The Elephant Man / $4.25
17743-6 RATTIGAN, TERENCE / Plays: One /. $5.95
17948-X SHAWN, WALLACE and GREGORY, ANDRE / My Dinner with André / $5.95
17884-X STOPPARD, TOM / Travesties / $3.95
17260-4 STOPPARD, TOM / Rosencrantz and Guildenstern Are Dead / $3.95
17206-X WALEY, ARTHUR, tr. and ed. / The No Plays of Japan / $7.95

GROVE PRESS, INC., 196 West Houston St., New York, N.Y. 10014